Make it Personal

Design and develo[p]
your own unique wo[rk]

GW00645080

Book 1: Preparing your Palette

By Hilary Beattie

Contents

Introduction

This book is the first in as series of books which will look at how to work through from inspiration to fully integrated work, in a simple, non-intimidating way. I am so often asked 'where do you get the ideas from?' or 'how do you get from photos to quilt?', that I decided this would be a useful series of books to write. I shall be taking popular themes and share all my thoughts and process from that first photo, or sketch, or idea, through to the completed work. I started doing this with a first theme for Book 1, and soon realised that much of my process work relies heavily on materials I have personally made for that specific theme. Indeed, much inspiration for design comes directly from this process. So I decided book one should really be about making our materials or preparing our palette.. Once we have that, we are good to go and can dive happily into design and making.

We are totally spoilt these days with a truly wonderful range of commercially produced fabrics and papers - probably more than at any time before. I suspect our frugal ancestors would not be able to believe their eyes. You can get plains, ditsy florals, modern geometrics, quirky prints, textural imagery, realistic imagery, abstract patterns, retro inspired and so the list goes on. You can get them in a mass of colourways and you can even get your own art work printed on to fabric - how fabulous is that? So why, with this extensive range to choose from, would you want to consider making your own materials?

Well ... consider these:

- they will be unique to you and every single piece will be different

- they will resonate with your personality and hand

- they have a multi-layered look and complexity you just cannot get any other way

- you will gain an understanding of your subject and a great deal of inspiration for designs as you work on producing your palette

- colours, patterns and sizes - all the choices are yours and yours alone

- they are just huge fun to produce!!

And you don't have to ignore all those lush and tempting commercial options either. Indulge yourself a little and try combining your purchased materials with your hand-made ones for a gloriously eclectic and lively look. This seems to me to be the best of both worlds - so why settle for anything less?

I use both fabric and paper in my design work and in finished pieces. If you have never tried adding paper elements into your work, I would encourage you to have a go — they add a different textural quality to the work and I love to see the combination of both materials. Obviously, if you want to wash a piece, paper may not be such a good plan! However, sealed with matt medium, it is surprisingly tough, and will certainly cope with being wiped down. Even if you do not want to put paper in your finished work, it is still worth preparing some papers when making your materials, as they are invaluable for collage and design exercise in your sketchbook.

In chapter one, we will look at materials we will be using and then in the remaining chapters I will take you through my favourite techniques for getting pattern and colour onto fabric and paper, in a fairly detailed way. I do very little according to 'the book' - whatever that book is. I tend to use techniques as they seem useful to me, and ignore any rules that aren't important for me.

So this is not a truly technical manual - there are many of those on all the techniques we will cover and I will list my favourites at the end of the book.

I am not knocking doing things the right way either - it all depends on what you want to achieve. I am very rarely looking for perfection, so I don't need to worry about rules that a professional fabric printer might follow. I'm making my own, eccentric cloth, so I use my own, rather irreverent techniques for doing things. Sometimes there is much to be said for a childlike innocence when creating. We can get too bound up in, and even intimidated by rules and procedures, the 'right' ways of doing things, and end up doing nothing as it seems so complicated. This is not good!! At the end of the day, we are applying colour to fabric and paper, not building a rocket! and it is actually quite hard to go wrong. So we will be looking at very simple ways to achieve our goal, always remembering that there is enough stuff in this world to worry about already and we don't need to add something so enjoyable to the list!!

So, let's get going, relax, enjoy ourselves and make a gorgeous, unique and personal palette.

Materials

You have probably noticed that we are somewhat spoilt with our choice of materials theses days - even the supermarket sells art stuff now! This is both a blessing (yummy shopping and stuff to hoard) and a curse (the hoard gets too big and the credit card looks a little sick). So rather than tell you all about everything there is, which you probably already have a fair bit of already, I am going to share with you my favourite stuff. I am trying very hard to downsize the number of products I need to store, so I find it useful to use one product for as many applications as possible. Each chapter lists in detail what is needed for that specific technique, so here we will look at our basic supplies.

Paints: I use fabric paints on both fabric and paper, as it means I only need one range of products. I also know that work on both materials will match in colour if I want it to. My favourite brand of fabric paints are Setacolour Opaque by Pebeo. They are not the cheapest, but their pigmentation and opacity is excellent, so I can use them on dark as well as light surfaces and know they will still be bright. They need heat setting with an iron if you want them to be washable. I don't usually require this, but I do like them to be water resistant so I can flood dyes over them, so I always heat fix them when using on fabric. I cannot pretend that I am never tempted by cheap acrylics and these Artiste craft paints are excellent and also come in a mouth-watering range of shades. Not that I have them all of course!

Dyes: I use procion mx dyes on both fabric and paper. They work on all natural fabrics, although I use mainly cotton. The only other products I use with them are soda ash as a fixative and manutex as a thickener (see next page for manutex) I pre-soak all my fabric in a soda ash solution (9 tbsps/lit - I use a lidded bucket with this ratio written on the lid) and then line dry them. I keep these separately so I know that when I want to work with dye, my fixative is already in there. Just be careful when you are ironing these fabrics, as the soda ash can make them singe and don't dry them in the tumble dryer! I make my liquid dyes in snap lid pots, mixing about 1 tsp. of dye powder with a small amount of hot water. Top this up to approx. 200 mls with water. You should wear a mask when handling the powder, as it is toxic if inhaled. Mix this up and you have an ink for your papers and dye for your cloth.

Applicators: I love big fat brushes for applying dyes as they hold a lot of liquid and puddle nicely when applied. I use sponge rollers extensively for applying paint to stamps, stencils, print plates and direct to cloth/paper. The small ones from the DIY store are good and often come with a little tray too. I have a selection of squeegees for using with screens and also to spread my thickened dye. My least favourite are actually the posh screen printing ones. I prefer a smaller spreader or credit card - easier to control I find.

Pencils and crayons: I couldn't be without these. They are brilliant for design and sketchbook work as well as for adding extra colour to your materials. I like to have a

combination of water resistant and As far as crayons go, Neocolour by gorgeous and wonderful quality. and Neocolour 2 water-soluble. I both. There is more choice with good. I love the inktense water-soluble and I use Faber Castel Polychromos as Again, I would get a good range of

water soluble in both products. Caran d'Ache are just Neocolour 1 are water resistant would get a good range of pencils and many ranges are pencils as they are so vibrant my water resistant pencils. colours in each type.

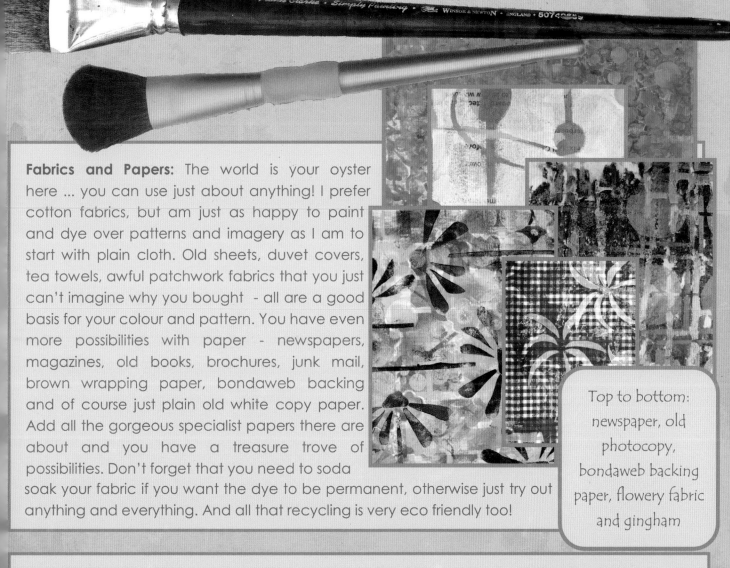

Fabrics and Papers: The world is your oyster here ... you can use just about anything! I prefer cotton fabrics, but am just as happy to paint and dye over patterns and imagery as I am to start with plain cloth. Old sheets, duvet covers, tea towels, awful patchwork fabrics that you just can't imagine why you bought - all are a good basis for your colour and pattern. You have even more possibilities with paper - newspapers, magazines, old books, brochures, junk mail, brown wrapping paper, bondaweb backing and of course just plain old white copy paper. Add all the gorgeous specialist papers there are about and you have a treasure trove of possibilities. Don't forget that you need to soda soak your fabric if you want the dye to be permanent, otherwise just try out anything and everything. And all that recycling is very eco friendly too!

Top to bottom: newspaper, old photocopy, bondaweb backing paper, flowery fabric and gingham

You will also need the usual supplies: scissors, craft knives, cutting mat, pencils, rubber, tracing paper and a sketchbook or loose paper for doodling and designing on. And that is it!   The number of ways you can use these materials is truly amazing. We will have a quick look at preparing dyes for printing and then we can get started with some ideas for using all this lovely stuff.

Mixing and Using Thickened Dye

You will need: print paste - this is easy to make. Fill a jug with water and sprinkle manutex powder over the top. I use 3 tbsp/litre and this makes a really thick paste. Whisk it up thoroughly and don't worry that it looks a vile lumpy mess right now. Leave for a few hours or overnight and it will have miraculously transformed in to a smooth gloopy paste. You also need: dye powder; a small pot to mix in (I like a jug as it is easy to pour the dye into the bottles after mixing); squeezy bottles or other containers with secure lids; a mask to wear when handling the powders in dye form as they are toxic when air borne (it's a pain, but just do it!); measuring spoon or teaspoon and other spoons/sticks for mixing.

Pour some of that gloopy paste in to your little jug/container.

Sprinkle some dye powder on the top. I use approx. 1 tsp/150mls which gives me a strong colour. I keep saying approx. as it really is. I don't worry much about exact quantities and you don't need to either. If I put less in, it is a bit lighter, and if I put more in it's a bit darker. I am happy to go with whatever I get, knowing that I can always go back in again with more dye/paint if I am not happy.

Now give it a really good mix up. If it seems too thick (unpourable), add a bit of water to the mix and stir very thoroughly.

Decant into your container and label ... this is helpful and even I try to do it! Use a waterproof pen like a sharpie or it will soon disappear. I also like to fill a container with plain print paste, which I can then use with the coloured pastes to lighten the colour if required.

Squeeze or spoon out some dye paste onto your cloth - you can put more than one colour on if you wish and also add plain paste to lighten if

desired. Use your squeegee (I love these ones from the DIY store) and pull the dye across your fabric. I am going over a previously paint printed fabric which is resisting the colour: we will be doing lots of that later!

The dye now needs to stay damp on the cloth (batch) for at least four hours. If you are working over fabric paint, you need to have heat fixed this with an iron before adding the dye, or it will break down a little - there again, that may be just what you want. I fold and put the cloth into plastic bags and stack them up in a tray to batch. When the time is up, rinse out all the excess dye and print paste and enjoy your wonderful creation.

Stamps

Making your own stamps is one of the easiest and quickest ways to get going when starting to pattern your own materials. There are many ways of producing stamps to use, including string, heat mouldable blocks and lino-cutting.

All work very well, but I am going to concentrate here on cutting simple craft foam stamps which are quick, easy, cheap and very effective.

Foamboard, adhesive craft foam sheet, scissors and/or craft knife, ruler, pencil, tracing paper, paints, rollers, nice fat paint brushes, procion dyes, papers and fabric which should be treated with soda ash (see materials chapter for details)

Designs for these can be random or simple imagery. As long as you can cut it out, it's fine. I like to use shapes, patterns and simple forms, taken from my source subject. Sit with a sheet of paper, draw some boxes and just doodle ideas. Fill the boxes. Lines - straight or curved, flowers shapes, circles, leaves, houses, dots, swirls - the list is endless. Try and develop a habit of noticing simple shapes when you are out and about ... brick and paving patterns, shadows of plants, ripples in the water, patterns in nature, the weave on a basket - inspiration is truly everywhere when you start to look. Take photos for reference and then treat yourself to a cup of tea and a sketching session. No one needs to see this - it is for your benefit and eyes only.

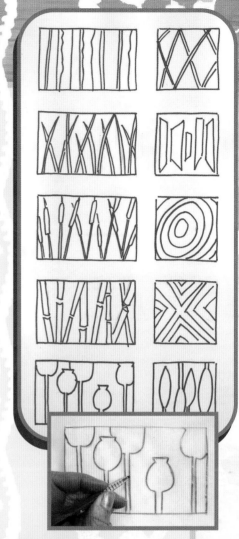

So choose a favourite design, or two and trace the pattern. Don't forget you can enlarge and reduce your design using a photocopier

Making the stamp

I often make a positive and a negative stamp. It uses the materials efficiently and is so useful when making patterns and designs. So trace two outlines onto your foam board and one onto your foam. Cut out the foam using scissors or a knife, and adhere the image to one piece of board and the background to another. Voila - you have a set of stamps.

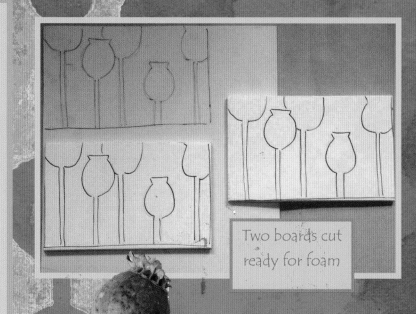

Two boards cut ready for foam

Positive (top) and negative bottom) stamps

Using your choice of paint, apply some to the stamps using a roller or a foam brush and make a test print of each

Using a single stamp for all over design

Apply paint to your stamp and start printing – always start just off the edge so you can use the whole piece

Then carry on printing until you've covered the sheet. I've rotated the block a few times for added interest

I've changed to a different stamp too … but I do get bored quickly!

Now add a second colour

and even a third if you fancy …

Don't bother changing your palette or roller— It all adds more interest!

Let the paint dry - this does not take long - heat fix with an iron and then add some dye on top .

Spread a mix of dye colours over the printed patterns – this is like watching magic … – honestly

Printing with positive & negative stamps

Here I have stamped the poppy design in repeats, alternating the positive and negative for an all over design

Adding dye

With this one, I've used red and gold together, making prints using positive and negative stamps printed over one another. I've also tried flipping the stamp and different offsets for the over print.

It is a good idea to keep half your piece un-dyed and dye the other half, for materials that will work beautifully together

I then slightly altered the design, made a stamp and printed some 'feature' pieces to go with the other poppy backgrounds

Printed and over-dyed as before

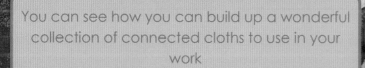

You can see how you can build up a wonderful collection of connected cloths to use in your work

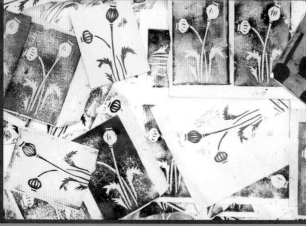

15

Designs need not be complicated to look very effective, especially when you play with the positive and negative spaces

If you fill cloth with imagery that coordinates, you can then pick out the bits you like and designing is so easy

Don't forget that you can photocopy simple leaf and flower shapes. This leaf was copied and printed in two different sizes, then many designs were tried out on both paper and fabric. Here the stamps have been used for some quite direct 'feature images' as well as backgrounds. They are truly versatile.

It can also be useful to cut a left facing and right facing stamp, as with these poppies. This opens up even more options.

A simple stamp has been used in a repeat pattern to make a long yardage of custom cloth. The pattern was taken from a vintage shoe strap and the cloth used to make a quilt about the shoes ... how nice is that?

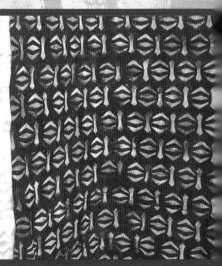

What About and What If ?

What about starting a sketchbook for patterns you see and committing to finding a new pattern every day? It will be brilliant for this and many other things too

What about making yourself a set of quirky alphabet or number stamps?

What if you printed with all white and then add colour only with dye?

What about making stamps in many different sizes of the same images and playing to see what you get? Try adding a small positive to a larger negative and vice versa

What about just chopping up foam sheets into random pieces and sticking them down randomly for background patterns?

What about making stamps of your pets? Or your family? Just take photos and trace the outlines

What if you make really large stamps? (you can get foam up to A3)

What if you print with aqua wax, or transparent acrylic and then wash dye over?

What about using coloured or patterned papers and fabrics and stamping over them?

What about taking photos of the stamps when they get covered in paint and using them printed out on paper or fabric for design/pieces too? They can get really gorgeous!

What about making matching stencils and stamps and seeing how they work together? But we haven't talked about stencils yet have we? So let's do that right now ...

Stencils

Another very simple and low-tech way to add pattern, imagery and colour to your fabrics and papers is by using stencils

You don't need much to make a stencil either. An image which you can translate to a simple line drawing, some plastic or even paper and a knife and you are good to go. In fact, you could just tear the paper and not even need the knife!

As with stamping, there are different ways of making and using stencils, including freezer paper, found materials such as lace, torn paper edges as masks and many more. I am again going to concentrate on just my favourite and quick methods for decorating materials. I like to use acetate for my stencils as it is strong and durable and so lasts a long time. It can cope with me forgetting to clean it and being a bit rough in use, without collapsing. Many of you will remember the craze for stencilling houses in the late 1980's and I still have the stencils I made then ... not bad. You can use thick acetate especially designed for stencils, or OHP transparencies, or even plastic file pockets cut open. All are cheap and all will work well.

I use basically two types of stencils - those I have designed and cut myself to complement a specific theme and also commercially made ones with a generic sort of a pattern, which I find really useful for making all over patterns and backgrounds.

Materials you will need:

Acetate or plastic sheet, stencil cutter or knife, cutting board or glass sheet (sealed around the edges), sanding block, paints, palettes, procion dyes, rollers, brushes, foam brushes, own designs, commercial stencils, soda soaked fabric (see materials section) and papers

Making your own stencil

Stencils are really just simplified line drawings, which use bridges to make sure all the pieces join together. You can use many things for inspiration - let yourself just sit and sketch out some ideas and thoughts. This lot were done on A5 paper, which I always carry in my bag, whilst sitting having coffee in the garden centre. I can bring these home and use my books or the internet to check details. I keep all stuff like this in a big envelope file labelled 'designs'. It is one of my most used files. I just stuff anything and everything in it.

adapting sketchbook work with shell patterns to design a stencil

take photos to help you get the shapes right - or if possible, trace around the object, as with this red maple leaf

you can make a stencil of just the outline shape , as on the left, but it is often more interesting to divide the shape up into areas, as on the right.

I have used the vein lines to guide me and then coloured in the pattern pieces to see how it will look. Don't forget you can re-size on the photocopier, either to get a size to suit, or to create a selection of sizes to work with. This makes creating layered and dynamic patterns alot easier.

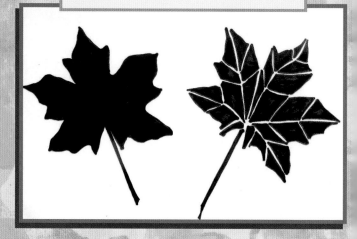

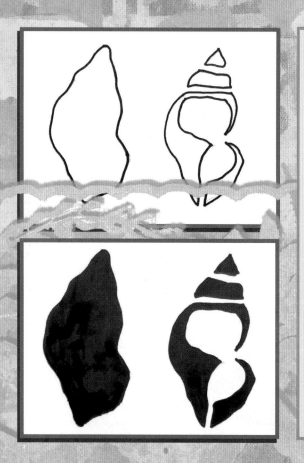

You will find that some shapes, such as the shell at left, just do not work well as a plain outline - they need some extra detail. Look carefully at the subject for clues to guide you. Here I have used a photo of the shell and traced my design from that.

Acetate can be cut with either a sharp craft knife, or a hot stencil tool. I find the latter very easy to use, but have also cut many stencils with a knife … so choose what suits you and your budget best. I like to use a sheet of glass to cut on as it allows me to place my design underneath and then cut the acetate on top. Always tape the edges of glass and have a sturdy pot to put your hot cutter in when resting (if using).

You may find the hot cutter leaves a slight burr on the surface of the acetate (especially if the sheet is thick). This can be removed with a fine sanding block – and your stencil is ready to use .

I've decided I am going to go with a seaside theme and use images of shells and crabs and ladders, together with the shell pattern as a larger background stencil

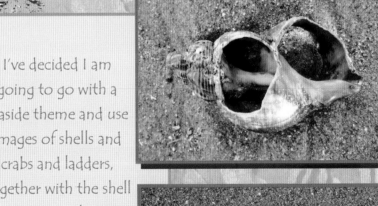

You can buy specialist stencil brushes, and these can be great for very fine or light work. I prefer to use either foam dabbers if I want to be a bit selective, or sponge rollers, as they are so quick!

Put your paint on your palette and get your roller nicely coated, but not dripping. That said - I often do a blobby print or two because I have too much paint on the roller, and it simply does not bother me. Put your stencil on the fabric and lightly roller over it.

Don't forget you can put more than one colour on the roller at a time.

You will find your own preferences for the amount of paint and the roller pressure as you work, but honestly, just enjoy the process. Remember we are making materials, not finished products here, so celebrate the imperfections of a truly handmade piece.

Lift the stencil and voila – a print!

Now - just keep going! You can use repeats with the stencil to make all over patterns, either in straight lines, drop repeats or changing the direction of the print (see recommendations at the back for a wonderful book about pattern printing)

Don't forget to print the negative

Add second and third layers of colour

You will build up wonderful, complex patterns

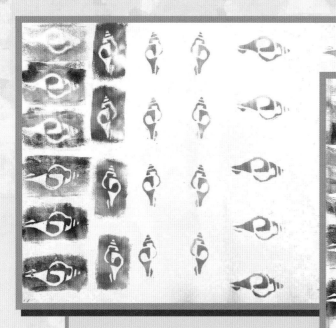

negative prints

You can use the stencils to make some potential feature or focal pieces. I like to do lots of stuff on the same big piece, so I know they will work together well. When you have printed your stencil, if you turn it over and use a clean, hard roller to apply it to the fabric, you will get the negative print and not waste all that lovely paint. These are often as nice, if not nicer

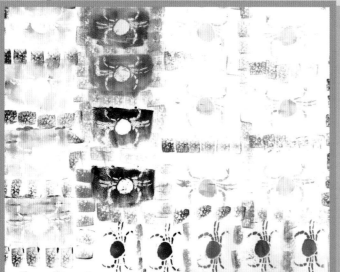

than the original, and the two will always work well together to add variety to your materials and work.

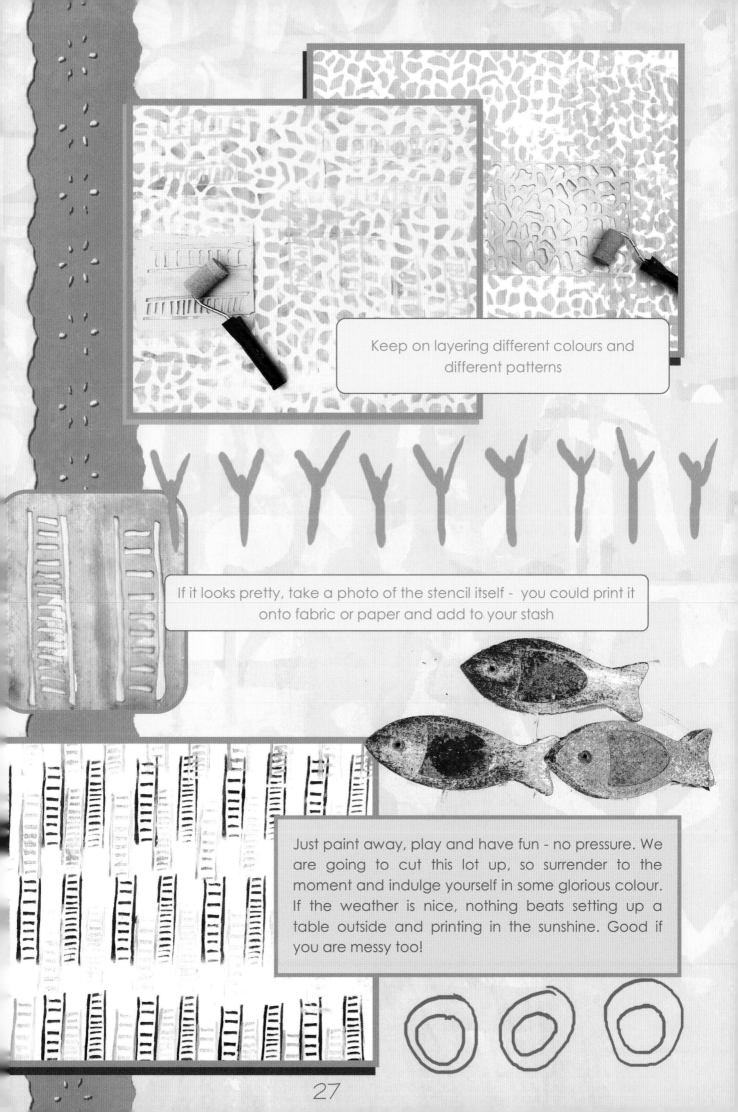

Keep on layering different colours and different patterns

If it looks pretty, take a photo of the stencil itself - you could print it onto fabric or paper and add to your stash

Just paint away, play and have fun - no pressure. We are going to cut this lot up, so surrender to the moment and indulge yourself in some glorious colour. If the weather is nice, nothing beats setting up a table outside and printing in the sunshine. Good if you are messy too!

Adding Dye

As before, I like to apply dye over my paint when it is dry, to give that gorgeous rich, multi- layered look. You don't have to, but I would definitely at least try it. I think you will probably be hooked. Remember you can always keep half and dye half.

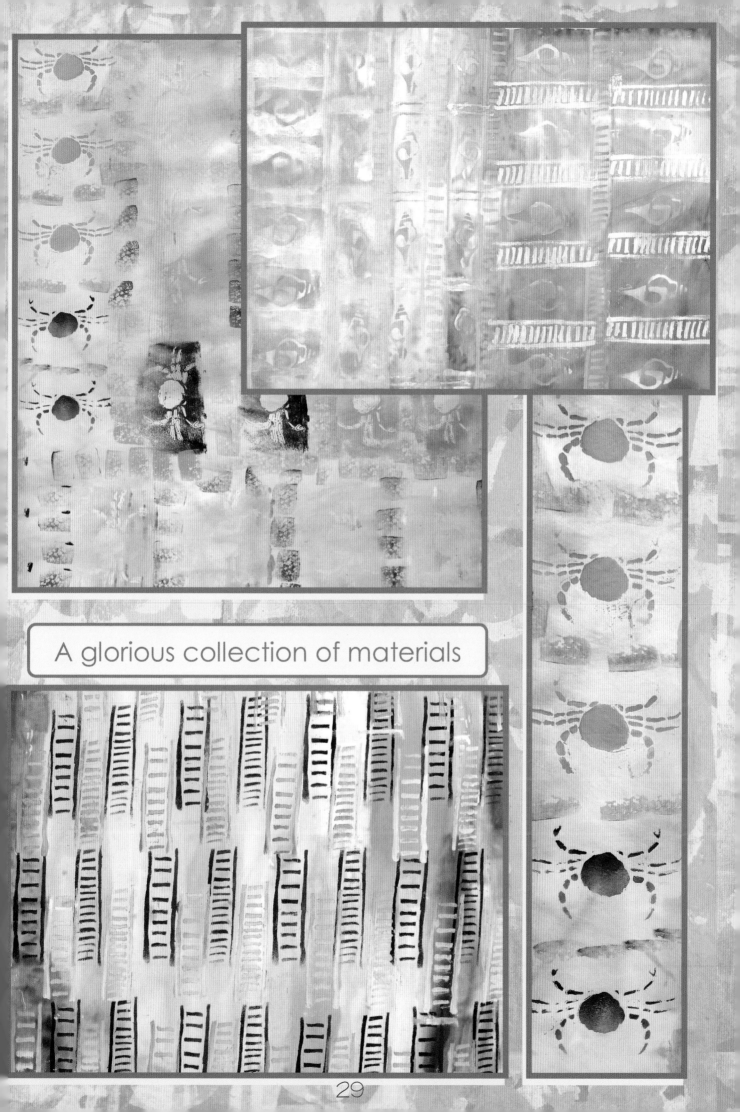

A glorious collection of materials

Using commercial stencils

So what about commercial stencils? Do we have to resist all those gorgeous designs out there in the name of integrity in our work? Hell - no!! Let's just use them with a bit of discretion. If I have a theme, then I like to make my own stencils for any direct imagery from my source of inspiration ... e.g. shells, leaves, trees, animals, flowers etc. These images are going to be important in the final piece and I want them to be my own. But when it comes to background patterns, I love to use good commercial stencils. Circles, squares, lines, letters, numbers swirls, lacy effects etc. I probably could cut them all myself, but it would take me a very long time and why bother when someone else has done such a nice job for me! I want to save my precious time for the more exciting bits. By the time we have layered and over-dyed these, we will have made the patterning truly our own ... so treat yourself to one or two.

Use the patterns in repeats, change the direction, turn them over, try using two different sizes and layer pattern on pattern. Then add dye. I promise you your result will be unique!

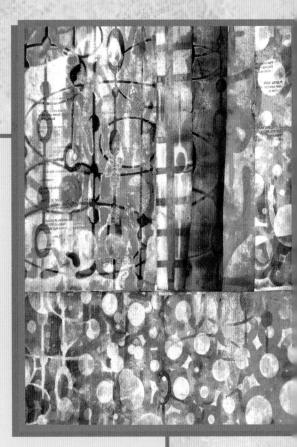

Piles of co-ordinating materials — all ready to use!!

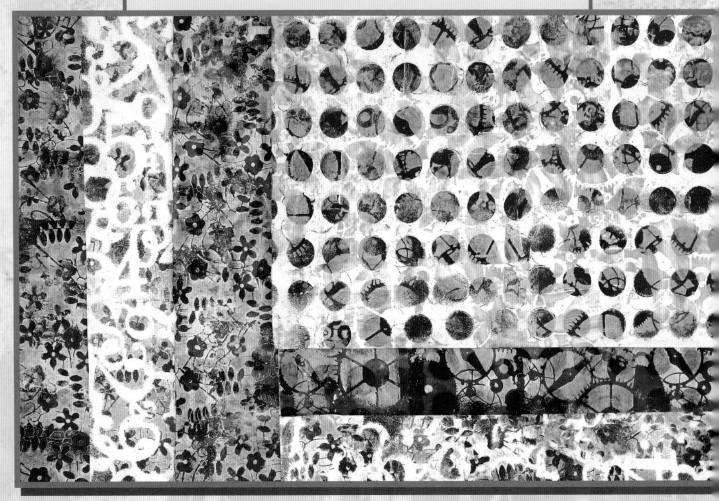

What About and What If?

- What about making a chequerboard of positive and negative prints and then over-dyeing for a piece almost ready to quilt?

- What about starting your own design file and putting some paper in your handbag? Jot down ideas whenever and wherever then put them in your file. You will be surprised how quickly it grows

- What about keeping a sketchbook handy when you are printing and using it for the negative prints and also to use up any spare paint? You will soon have a full book, with inspiring staring points on every page

- What about drawing through your stencils with waterproof pen to make outline drawings and then adding more paint and on dye on top?

- What if you made some stencils of words associated with your theme and use these in your designs, either in correct orientation or reversed?

- What about taking a photo of, and then making a stencil featuring your house and using it as the basis for some personal work?

- What about experimenting with image editing software on your computer to simplify a photo of your face and then make a stencil of the result? Try seeing what some off the artistic effects do.

- What if you applied acrylic wax, clear liquitex or clear acrylic medium through your stencils and then added dye over the top, for some unpredictable results?

- What if you made rubbing plates to match your stencils and used them together? But we haven't talked about rubbings yet have we? So lets do that next ......

Rubbings

I remember doing rubbings at school, either at the church, using the tombstones or outside, using tree bark. Way back then I found it magical how you could transfer pattern from textured surfaces to your paper, and I still do. You can of course still go and make rubbings of tree bark, pavements, drain covers, bricks, stone and all the other interesting textures you will find in the world around you. But it is quite a task and you will get some funny looks, so I prefer these days to make my rubbings indoors, using a combination of natural materials and plates I have designed and then made myself

As with previous techniques, you can use rubbings to make overall background patterns, or to produce feature pieces which may became the focal points of your work. I like to do both and produce a lovely set of materials that work well together and make designing my work so much easier.

Materials you will need;

Thick cardboard, scissors, sharp knife, cutting mat, appliglue, double sided tape or glue, designs, tracing paper, water resistant crayons, procion dyes, paper and soda soaked fabric

Designs for rubbing are really quite similar to those for stamps and stencils. We want clear outlines and some interesting shapes. In addition, by using appliglue, we can make some lovely fine line designs too. Once again - allow yourself a bit of time and just sit and sketch out some ideas. These do not have to be brilliant; they are for your eyes only and are simply a way to work through your thoughts. My first tutor used to use the expression "thinking with a pencil", and I have never forgotten it. That is just the best way to think in terms of design.

Making a cardboard rubbing plate

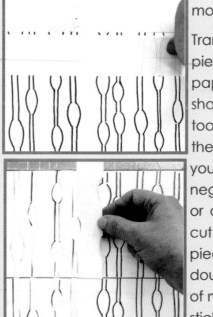

You will need fairly thick cardboard for this ... watch out in packaging and on the back of notepads for suitable pieces - mount board is excellent

Transfer your design to both pieces of cardboard using tracing paper. Cut out using scissors or a sharp knife. If your design is not too complicated, try and keep the negative design intact too, so you can make both a positive and negative plate. Using either glue or double sided tape, attach the cut out pieces on to your base piece of card. If you have used double sided tape, a quick coat of matte medium will get rid of the stickiness in the gaps and stop you sticking your plate to your fabric!

I've decided on a theme of tulips for my

rubbings, and I now want to make a feature plate. I remembered these paintings I did a year or two ago, for a quilt I made based on the piece of vintage fabric (inset).

I love that stylisation, so I've drawn up a similar sort of pattern using my tulips. As I want it to be reasonably symmetrical, I've just drawn half my pattern and then traced and transferred the other half to get a full design.

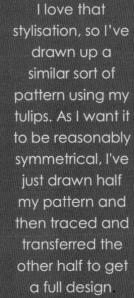

This was then traced, cut and mounted as with the other cardboard plate. I was very careful with my cutting, so that I would also be able to use the negative piece. Cut slowly and gently at first, and go over the line several times. Always use a really sharp knife - it makes such a difference. I like these ones with snap off blades … it makes it easy to change the blade, so you will be more likely to do it!

Don't forget you can resize your design using the photocopier

Remember to coat your plate in matte medium if it is sticky, otherwise your material will stick to it. I was too impatient here (a very common failing of mine) and couldn't wait to see how it would look, so tried a quick rubbing before I had coated it with medium. All that mess on the right hand side plate is where the paper stuck. Bad plan! - luckily it doesn't affect the plates usefulness, but a bit of a waste of time. So, do as I say and not as I do!!

Let the medium dry and cut the two plates apart. You are now ready to start making some gorgeous rubbings.

Making an appliglue rubbing plate

Appliglue is coloured, thick glue which comes in a useful little squeeze bottle. As you might guess it is glue, but we are going to use it to draw fine lines, which will make us some lovely delicate plates.

drawing delicate grasses with the appliglue

great for adding text too

Transfer your design to a piece of card using tracing paper. Have a practice on some spare paper to make sure the appliglue is running smoothly and to get a feel for how hard you need to squeeze. Then go over your design with the glue. Use a gentle pressure - you can always go back over it again. Leave until fully dry, the glue will then be hard to the touch.

Making a rubbing with your plate

Put the plate underneath your material and gently rub over it, using a water resistant crayon. My favourites are Neocolour 1 crayons, but markal and even kids crayons will work well. Work across the plate and adjust your pressure to see what different results you can achieve.

try using a second colour on the same rubbing

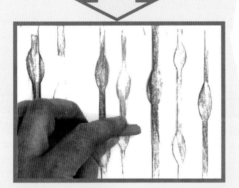

even a third →

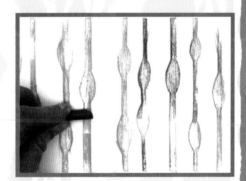

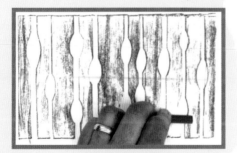

← don't forget the negative plates

Try using a candle or white crayon to make a rubbing. You will see nothing at this stage, but wait until we add some dye!

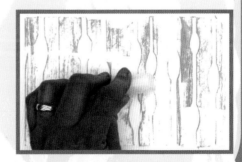

Making a rubbing with your appliglue plate

As before, put the rubbing plate under your material and with a very gentle touch, start to rub over the plate with your water resistant crayon. Add more pressure if needed, but this will be a more subtle, fine rubbing than with the cardboard plate.

You can use combinations of colour on the same plate

Here I have repeated the rubbing to make a long line of seed-heads

Just be careful and avoid rubbing the edges in between

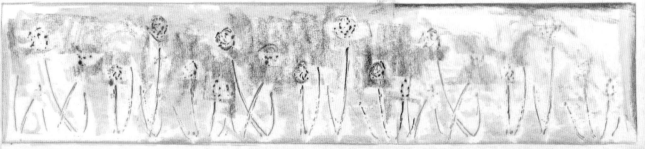

Adding dye

As with stamps and stencils, it is a bit magical when you add dye over the top of your rubbings.. Mix your dye colours as you work and watch how beautifully the wax crayon resists the liquid dye. Use a fat brush or a squeegee to spread the colour.

Here you can see how wonderful the white crayon and candle wax look when you add your dye

Lovely effects achieved with very simple patterns and variations of crayon and dye

Apply crayon lightly at first

Then apply more pressure to darken

As far as stamping and stencilling go, we use exactly the same techniques on paper and fabric, just varying the way we apply the dye (see materials section for information about dyes and application methods). Rubbings are a bit different as we are using neocolour 1 crayons, which are water-resistant, but not really washable in my experience. If you want a completely washable rubbing then the best plan would be to use markal oil sticks. But I don't like the smell or messiness (is it me?!) of these, so prefer to work around the limitations of the neocolour. Neocolour also come in many more colours and are somewhat cheaper as well. So here is my way of using them.

add a second

even third colour

Make your rubbing as thick as you can and leave the crayon to cure for a couple of days. Then heat set with an iron (use scrap paper on your ironing pad to catch the excess coloured wax which will come off). Then apply your dye, either with a very small amount of manutex thickener and a squeegee, or mixed just with water and using a thick paint brush. This will use quite a bit of dye, but you can help this by spraying your cloth first to dampen it and by dipping your paint brush intermittently into plain water to spread the colour. These application methods mean we will have very little if any paste to rinse out at the end.

use the crayons to add specific detail

Let your cloth dry and then leave it for a week or so for the dye to set (we are not damp batching in this case). Rinse quickly and lightly and hang to dry.

This method will give you a good rubbing effect, but do be aware

I like my thickened dye in squeeze bottles

that the cloth is not completely colour fast, so treat carefully. If you work like me, this is not a problem and I sometimes don't even bother rinsing the cloth if I have not used manutex.

If this all sounds a bit confusing or long winded (it certainly tries my patience!) then stick to paper for your rubbings — it is simper and the results are stunning I think. There are lots of other techniques we can use on fabric and we are going to mix both in our work, so it's not a problem.

Squeeze out one colour, then add another and scrape across

A wonderful cloth with rubbings and dye ... but it will need very gentle rinsing to keep this look

A glorious collection of rich, textural materials … makes my fingers itch to get creating!

When you have a
palette like this, the
possibilities are
simply endless

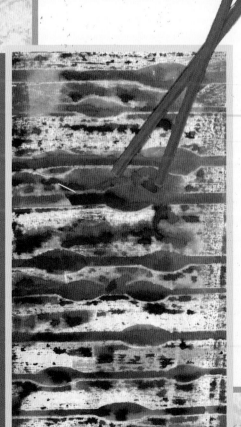

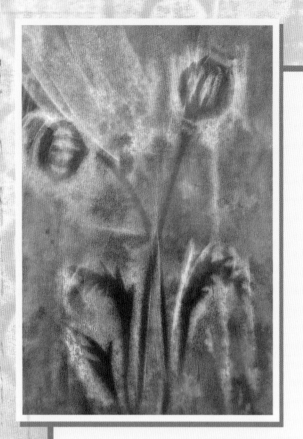

What if you made some rubbings using
your stamps (above) or stencils (below)
from previous chapters?

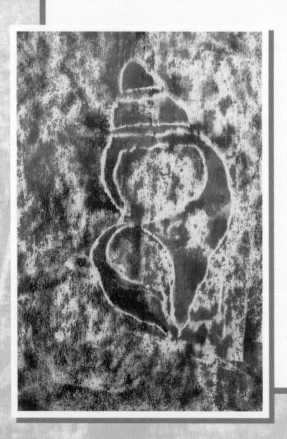

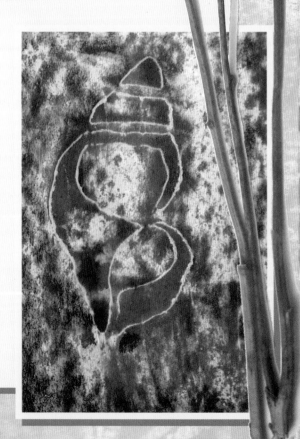

What About and What If?

- What about making rubbing plates that match or compliment your stamps and stencils and using them all together?

- What if you made all white rubbings and then washed over with black dye for a simple but dramatic look?

- What about going for a walk and collecting leaves, feathers, bark etc. to use for rubbings in your journal/sketchbook? What a lovely way to record the day

- What about making a rubbing plate of your name and using it as a quilt label on the back of your work?

- What if you made rubbing plates based on some of your favourite quilt blocks?

- What about going round your home and seeing how many different things you can find to take rubbings from? These could be the basis of some interesting work based on your own environment

- What if you made plates of the same image in both card and appliglue and tried overlaying them?

- What about having a good trip round your local art/crafts/ scrap booking and DIY store? You will find simply masses of things that could make great rubbings

- What about combining in rubbings with mono prints for some really textural materials? But we haven't looked at mono prints yet have we? ... so let's do that now .....

Monoprints

Monoprinting is a wonderful technique to add to your repertoire of skills for decorating your fabrics and papers. You will get texture and impressionistic images that you really could not achieve any other way. And every single one is unique ... try as you might, you will not be able to exactly replicate it, although you will make many more gorgeous prints in the attempt!

When trying them for the first time, lots of us have been a bit put off monoprints I think, as we have just made one plain print and it can look a bit, well ... boring! Sometimes one print is enough and it will make your heart sing and suggest all sorts of design possibilities to you. But more often, I find going back for second and even a third print livens things up. And then of course, if we make our prints using our acrylic or fabric paints, we can then go back over with dye ... and we know how exciting that can be don't we?

Materials: Sheet of acetate or glass with taped edges, sponge roller, hard roller, brushes, paints, palette, dye, mark making tools, images for inspiration

So let's look at what we need to get started

Mark making tools: patterned rollers, sponges, combs, sticks, tubes, palette knife, foam shapes, pipettes, cotton buds and anything else

Let's start by having a look at making patterned and textural monoprints and then move on to see how we can use some more direct imagery as well.

I like to use acetate as a print plate for most of my monoprints as it is easy to handle, cheap and I can keep the used sheets as extra materials in my palette. If I am working larger than A4, however, I find it easier to use a glass sheet for stability. If you do this, make sure to tape the edges very carefully to avoid cutting yourself.

You need to work fast to prevent the paint drying on the palette so have everything laid out and ready to go

Take your sheet of acetate or glass (print plate) and lay it flat. Roll out some paint on your palette and then apply to your print plate. You can use one colour, or mix them up a bit. You need to work quite fast as the paint will dry quickly, so as soon as you have your paint on the plate start to make marks into it using any

49

Lift your print plate and turn it paint side down onto your fabric or paper. Use the hard roller to go over and get good contact between the plate and your material. Lift your fabric and see what you have got. You may be lucky and have a little gem straight away. If so - brilliant.

Go over with a hard roller to ensure good contact

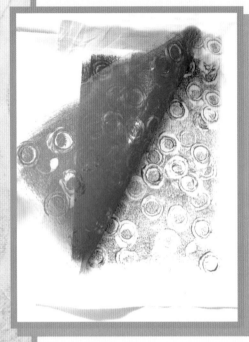

If however, you have a sort of 'alright but not very exciting print', like this

then do not worry ... 99 percent of mine are like that. Just put it aside to dry and then we will go back over it again.

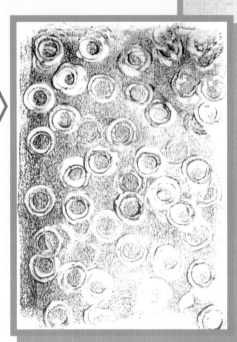

You may notice, as below left, that you have quite a lot of paint left on your palette. Rather than waste this - we don't like waste - lightly spray over the plate with water and print it off again. It will be a bit more 'splodgy', but still a useful print.

first print (left) and second (right)

print

used plate

50

this patterned roller gives this interesting print

Meanwhile, ink - well paint actually - up your print plate and make some more

Don't worry about cleaning your plate in between, you will get a bit of serendipity in your colours, but that is a good thing I think.

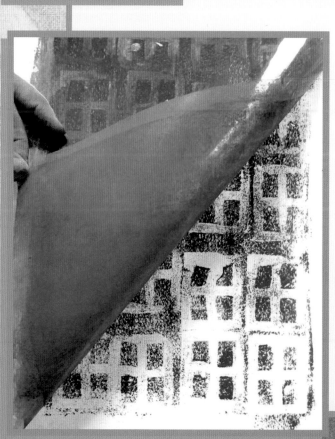

This (above right) is a foam piece from a childs game. Each time it is pressed onto the plate, it picks up paint. This will stop it picking up paint again as effectively, next time, so print it off onto a spare piece of material (insert) - it will clear the foam and give you an extra piece of cloth!

You can see (left) what a great print it made. See what you can find to make marks with

Using an old make-up applicator to draw hoops

and my favourite palette knife to draw some ladders. You need to write backwards and as you can see, I struggle with backward 'S' !

and a new use for a broken comb

So now we have nice pile of once printed materials. What about another layer? Choose another colour and roller it out on the plate. You might choose to stay close in colour range, using, for instance turquoise and blue, or you might fancy a real contrast, like blue and orange. I like to make roughly the same marks (this will really only be roughly, so don't worry) and then apply this on top of my first layer. Either print more or less on top of the first image or go for the gaps. Or both. And maybe add a third colour if it still looks a bit boring to you.

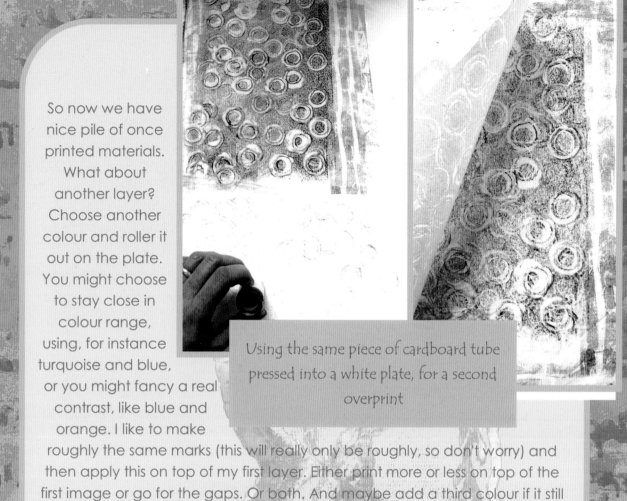

Using the same piece of cardboard tube pressed into a white plate, for a second overprint

More over-prints in white – one of my favourite combinations

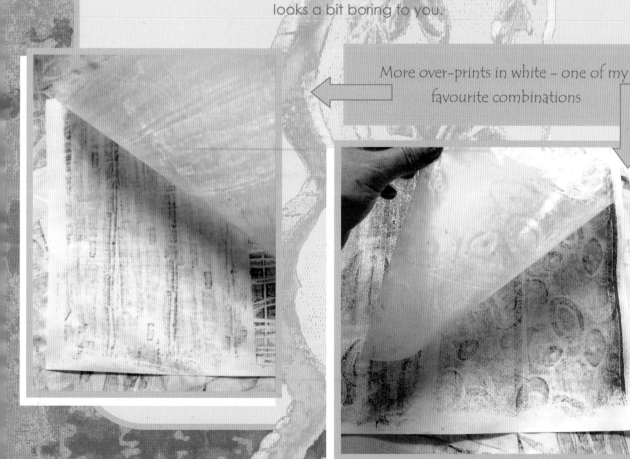

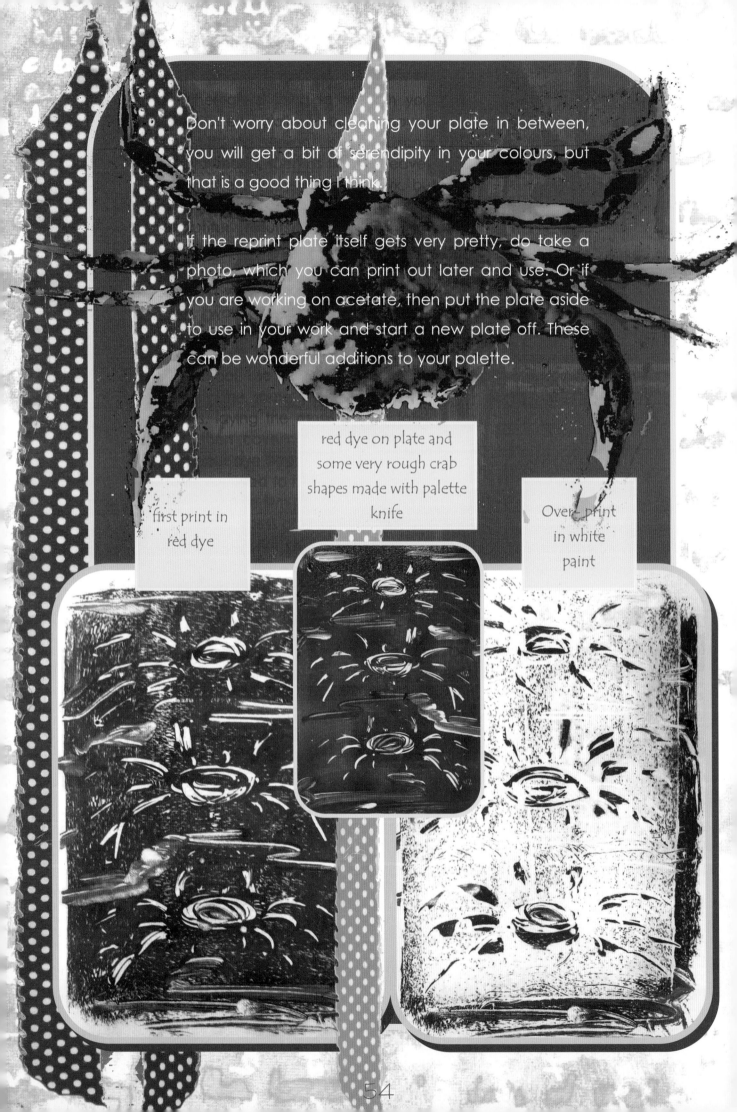

Don't worry about cleaning your plate in between, you will get a bit of serendipity in your colours, but that is a good thing I think.

If the reprint plate itself gets very pretty, do take a photo, which you can print out later and use. Or if you are working on acetate, then put the plate aside to use in your work and start a new plate off. These can be wonderful additions to your palette.

red dye on plate and some very rough crab shapes made with palette knife

first print in red dye

Over-print in white paint

first print in red dye then over print again in white paint

Keep printing until you have a nice pile of materials to add some dye to.

Once the paint is dry, you can start brushing or squeegeeing some dye over. As we have seen before this is quite magical and makes a huge difference to your pieces.

don't forget to use the iron to heat set your paint before adding wet dye

Truly
yummy
stuff!

So now we have made some lovely textural pieces with our fairly random mark making, let's move on and look at making some monoprints using more direct images.

I like to print up some photographs of things that interest me and that have good strong lines for printing. I then work with these by my print plate and make my marks using them as a guide.

A photo of birch trees in a local nature reserve inspired many prints in my sketchbook, on paper and on fabric. I layered dye and paint and worked on black as well as white grounds

Using hogweed as
inspiration (this page)
and some glass vases
(opposite page)

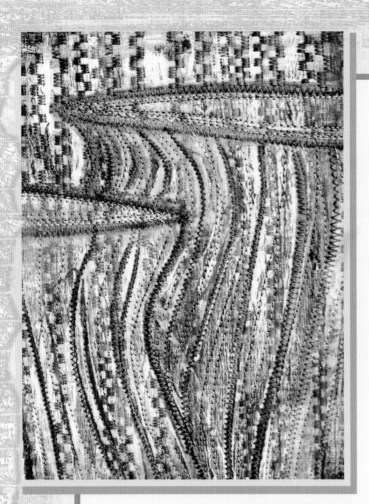

some of the monoprints with stitching added - the
prints give you easy lines to follow

What About and What If ?

- What about starting a scrapbook or album and collecting images that you think would provide good inspiration for monoprinting?

- What about allocating a box for keeping any objects you come across for making marks? Be warned, this can get a bit obsessional

- What about painting or dyeing some papers/fabrics first and then adding monoprints on top?

- What about setting up for a session in the garden and making marks on your plate inspired by what you see around you?

- What about pressing shoe soles into your plate for some shoe print pieces?

- What if you press your hand or foot onto the plate? Messy I know, but could be the basis for some fascinating personal work and I always get messy anyway

- What if you pressed your stamps or rubbing plates onto your monoprint plate? You might get some interesting connected materials

- What about drawing an object on your print plate with your non-dominant hand and then printing it off? Maybe repeat a few times for a quirky series of images

- What if you photographed one of your favourite prints, changed it to black and white and had a thermofax screen made from it? But we haven't talked about screen printing yet have we? So lets move straight on and do that now ...

Screen Printing

Well here we are then, at our last technique for now. And what technique it is! Screen printing is a huge subject, with whole books written about it (see bibliography for some excellent ones). But its very vastness can make it seem a little intimidating. I can still remember the first time I had a go .... my paint didn't get through the screen, everything splodged and the results were lacklustre to say the least. It put me off for a while; I felt it was just too complicated for me. But I'm so glad I tried again, because it does not have to be complicated at all - it can be very simple and still give stunning results. So that is what we are going to look at in this chapter. A few very simple ways of using screens, to put your own patterns and imagery onto cloth and paper.

Let's start by looking at what equipment you need - and don't worry ... It is not much.

Materials:

Screen/s - the easiest and most reliable method to get these is to buy them from one of the suppliers listed at the back of the book. You can make your own, but it is a job that needs to be done right, so I just support other screen makers. Size-wise, I would go for about A4 size or a 10" ish square. A smaller square is also useful, although you can change the size of your screen with masking tape. It is handy to have two or three screens to save a bit of time, but one will do for starters, and see if you enjoy the process.

Unless it comes ready varnished (which many now do) you will need to either varnish all the exposed wood with waterproof varnish or cover the wood with duck tape. Just put the tape over all exposed wood. It is also useful to take the tape over the edge of the screen to give a small 'well' to put your paint/dye in. That said, my varnished screens don't have that and I have never found it a problem. Again there are many excellent books around which give detailed instructions on this, but don't stress over it. The worst that will happen is that your wood will get a bit wet when you wash the screen and therefore not last as long ... not the end of the world!!

Squeegee - although I have some lovely professional speedball squeegees, I really prefer using a smaller tool. My favourites are a pack of spreaders I got from the DIY and I also like using credit cards. I find these much easier and I just go over my screen as often as needed to cover it. Look at tile and grout spreaders!

We are also going to look at thermofax screens, but I'll talk a bit more about them when we get to that bit.

That's it for special equipment - not too bad eh? You will also need thickened dye (see materials section for instructions), fabric paint and a space to work which leaves you a spot to put down your screen away from your work. I say this although I frequently put my screen on my work and do get splodges as a result. This doesn't bother me, but if you do as I say not as I do you won't get them! I'd also have a nice roll of paper towels handy - but that is true of everything we are doing. Fabric and paper and you are ready to go

Printing using paper as a stencil

This is a really easy and effective way of getting some wonderful patterns or images to print. You can cut any simple shape, but I quite like cutting into concertina folded paper like we used to do at school ... do you remember? To do this, take a piece of paper roughly the size of the opening in your screen and fold it one way then the other like a fan. You can draw a rough shape or just cut straight into the paper. I've cut a very rough half person, giving a line of dolls like i used to make many, many years ago. You

could cut half a flower, an animal or a pattern (remember making snowflakes like this?) Just remember you need to keep some of the fold intact and the shape needs to be reasonably symmetrical. Open out your paper and you have a stencil, or more accurately, a mask to use with your screen.

Lay your mask flat on your material and place the screen over the top. Squeeze some dye or paint in a line along the top of the screen, then take your squeegee, and with a good firm pressure, pull the colour across. You can make several pulls to cover the screen and go over a few times to make sure the dye or paint has gone through. This is particularly useful with the first print as the dry screen can need a bit more dye or paint to penetrate than when it is wet. It is actually very easy to see where the colour has and hasn't gone - there will be a white or pale gap visible. So just go back over and add more dye/paint as needed.

Lift your screen and you will have a

See that gap?

print - hopefully a good clear one.

Don't worry though if not - just go to another area of cloth or paper and print again. And don't discard those duffer prints either... I generally have quite a few splodgy ones, as I work fast and do tend to make a mess. But these prints, whilst not perfect, are still very usable, either as is with some stitch added, or as a basis for more imagery/ colour. We will talk more about that in the next chapter. But back to screens now.

Feel free to change the colour on your screen to add interest. I don't bother cleaning the screen in between, that way I get lovely mixes and gradual colour changes, which I think looks really interesting. You can also add more than one colour at a time and pull both across for a multi-coloured look. You can print with either dye or fabric paint, but when using the paint, do try and make sure you don't let it dry on the screen as it is very hard/impossible to get back out. I sometimes put a tray of water next to my workstation, so I can drop the screen into it when I am finished. As with other techniques, I like to combine dye and paint, sometimes starting with dyes and then adding paint on top, sometimes starting with paint and then adding dye over that, and often both! Try lots of things and see what looks good.

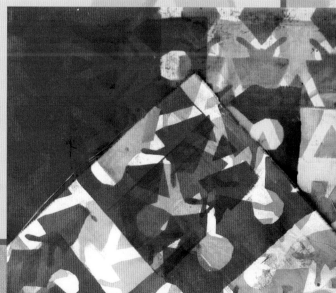

Leftovers from the Region 10 banner ... free stencils!!

trees chosen

A wonderful source for paper stencils to use with your screens is the backing paper from your applique shapes when using bonded applique. Keep these backing papers in a labelled file and get them out when you are planning a screening session. I had a whole pile left when I made a banner for my guild region and was thrilled with some of the prints I got from using these 'waste' pieces. They won't last for more than one session and will fall apart fairly quickly. But so what?? You will still get plenty of yummy pieces of material I promise!

screen laid over stencil

an inspiring
collection

Another great thing to try with your screens, especially if you are having an outdoor session, is using some natural masks, such as flowers, leaves, feathers etc. They won't all work, but many will and you will get some beautiful results. You will need materials that aren't too thick, or the screen will not be able to make contact with your cloth or paper. But as ever, I would say give it a go if you fancy it, you have nothing to lose except a bit of dye and fabric ... and we will use those too! Use your natural mask in exactly the same way as the paper masks, laying the mask on the fabric and then covering with the screen. Add your dye or paint and pull across. You may need to make several passes and use quite firm pressure, depending on the thickness of the mask you have chosen. Re-print as you wish, layering dye and paint as you fancy. These prints are unlikely to be as clear as with paper masks, and the natural mask may well deteriorate as you print ... but that just adds more texture and interest. Don't forget to keep the ones that haven't worked so well - they will definitely come in for something.

three thistle leaves ... a lovely shape and what a great way to use them!!

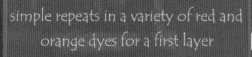

simple repeats in a variety of red and orange dyes for a first layer

after allowing the dye to dry a little, I am now adding square prints using more thistle leaves with blue paint

once the paint layer is dry, I ironed to fix it and then scraped yellow dye over half the piece and kept half plain as a good contrast

trying with a piece of geranium … you can see it is very
frail and only managed one print - but quite a nice one

I found a tougher plant, an herbaceous potentilla
… it took a bit of effort to get the dye to make
contact with the cloth behind it, but I'm really
pleased with the result - it looks very organic to
me

repeat prints (below) which were then over-dyed (left and left below)

this one is so lovely in blue and white, I have resisted dyeing it (so far!)

73

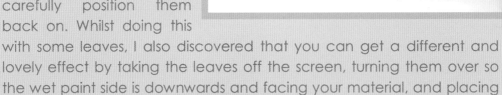

You may find that the leaves/flowers etc. tend to come off the screen a bit more easily than the paper mask did. If this does happen, you can just carefully position them back on. Whilst doing this with some leaves, I also discovered that you can get a different and lovely effect by taking the leaves off the screen, turning them over so the wet paint side is downwards and facing your material, and placing them on the fabric/paper. Then put your screen over and add a different colour of dye/paint. Pull across and lift. Peel the leaves off the material, turn them over again and replace on a different spot on the fabric/paper. Once more adjust the colour in the screen and pull across. Lift off and repeat this process as often as desired.

the top of this cloth has been printed using leaves as a straightforward mask .. in white, so they will only show when we add dye. The leaves were then peeled off each time (above) and new prints made using a sienna colour (below)

here is the cloth after grey dye was added … you can see the extra texture in the leaf prints below, compared to the voided shapes above, which have now appeared

With this technique you get actual prints of the leaves, rather than just a void. Hard to explain - easy to do … have a go!

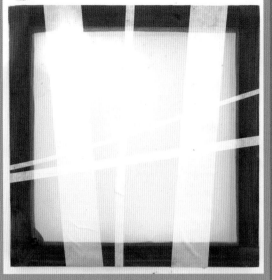

You are probably realising that we could go on for a long time

make use of different thicknesses of masking tape when preparing your screen

with rigid screens, but for now, just one more idea for the screens and then we will have a look at thermofax. I love using masking tape on my screen to mask off areas and provide wonderful background colour and pattern on my materials. This is so easy to do it is almost insulting! Take your screen and put strips of tape across the face (flat side). You can do this in one direction (stripes) or both (checks). You can make these even, or uneven, straight or diagonal and of different thicknesses. Once this is done – you are ready to print, just as before. The tape will last very well and if you are careful when you remove it, you could even keep the coloured strips as a collage element too.

I have layered many shades of dye from yellow to dark blue here

After allowing the cloth to dry a little, I have used the same screen (I stored it in a plastic bag to stop it drying out) and gone over in bright yellow and blue paints. Some dye must have dried and clogged the screen a little, as I have some patching in the top paint prints ... but you know by now that I'm not bothered don't you?! This combination of dyes and paints gives incredible depth to the material - you seem to be gazing through it

Once the paint was dry and heat fixed, I again added dye to half the cloth, producing two vibrant, co-ordinating materials

Here I have used masking tape from a wide roll and torn the edges. I've then placed them in random directions on the face of the screen. I've also put torn pieces around the edge to avoid a hard square surround on the print. The first layer is red and blue dyes, allowed to mix to produce some purples and burgundies on the material. After the dyes had dried I used a leaf from my purple elder with a square screen and printed over the top with blue paint. I wanted to see how the rather geometric background would work with a natural organic shape on top ... I think it works rather nicely. As with previous pieces, I over-dyed half and kept half the piece with the white background showing (below right)

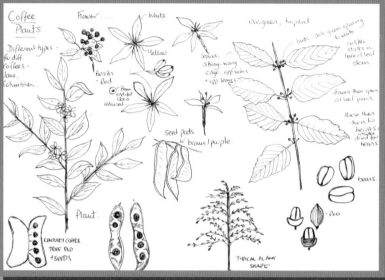

A thermofax machine works by burning a design into the mesh, wherever there is black toner. I recently bought my own machine from Germany and I just love it. But you don't have to do that. There are several suppliers of screens, who will custom burn one for you from your own black and white image. Design wise the possibilities are endless. Anything that you can draw, print or convert to black and white will work. Here you can see several options that I used for a recent theme of 'coffee' I drew coffee beans both solid and outline, I made a sheet of lettering using words associated with my theme. I also made my design sheet into a screen and then converted a photo of my coffee cup to black and white for another screen. Each can be burned as both a positive and negative and a left facing and right facing screen, not to mention in different sizes. You can see why I say endless possibilities!

If you buy thermofax screens, they will come in a nice neat plastic frame. As I make so many, I

don't bother with the frame and just edge my screens with duck tape (above). I find this works fine for me and it does mean the screen will bend around a surface should I want it to, and also they are thinner for storage. None of this need concern you if you are just buying a few screens for a particular project, but once you get into hundreds of screens, it does become an issue! You can use your screen with either dye or paint, but as before, be very aware of the paint drying out and make sure you clean your screen or put it to soak before this happens. Spread your medium of choice on the duck tape or plastic surround and pull it over the screen using a squeegee of some sort. I like a small one for this, a credit card is ideal.

then adding red and letting the two mix

80

a negative screen is printed in various colours and overprints (left) and then the positive screen of the same imagery is also used over the cloth (below)

Keep the pressure a bit lighter - these are not such thick brutes as the silk screens we have been using. I quite often use a sponge roller with my thermofax screens and this works really well too. You can mix your colours, overprint and generally enjoy yourself as before. Play with different sizes and positive/negatives if you have them - these are very design friendly screens.

❌ ❌ ❌ ❌ ❌

The same process but with the coffee bean screen this time. After the paint was dry, I heat set it with an iron and then over-dyed half of each cloth with red/brown (below left) and green (below right). I love these cloths.

What About and What If?

- What if you made a paper mask to give a circular shape to the screen and then put masking tape over that and printed circles all over your cloth?

- What about making some pieces in single colours, from light to dark, just adding a little more of the darkest colour with each print? You could build a wonderful palette of basic colours like this.

- What about making a print with any of your rigid screen techniques, photographing it and then altering it to black and white to use as a thermofax design? Make or have it made in different sizes and then print your materials with both silk and thermofax screens.

- What about taking some flowers or foliage from a special bouquet and using them to print material to make into a long term keepsake? How nice would that be for a wedding or special anniversary?

- What about altering a photograph of yourself/ your family or favourite pets into black and white and getting some thermofax screens made? These would make great prints for special pieces of work.

- What if you tried a paper doily or some fine lace as a mask with the screen? You might get some stunning effects

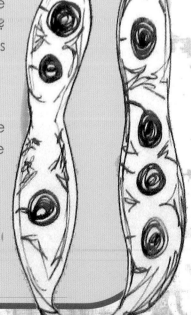

Pulling it all Together

What about the duffers??

Hopefully you now have a big pile of unique personal materials to use in your design and finished work. Hopefully too, you have thoroughly enjoyed the process of acquiring that pile. Some bits will be outstanding triumphs and you will be itching to get going with them. But what about the ones that just don't really cut the mustard?

Well first up: don't underestimate the usefulness of a piece, just because it doesn't

make you swoon with delight as a whole. For a lot of our design work and indeed in our finished work, we are going to be cutting/ tearing our pieces into smaller parts, and that is often a lot easier with bits you haven't fallen in love with as a whole cloth. It is also surprising how effective smaller parts become as you crop, tear and strip your materials. Remember, we don't need a whole palette of stars. In fact, we need relatively few centre piece/ focal point materials. We need an awful lot more of the chorus ... and that is where the also-rans are invaluable. Have look at the following photos of collages made using handmade papers and fabrics.

These collages in my sketchbook have been made using some of the materials opposite. If you look closely at the individual bits, they are not all gorgeous on their own and very few would cope with centre stage. But chop them up and put them together again and things really start to get exciting.

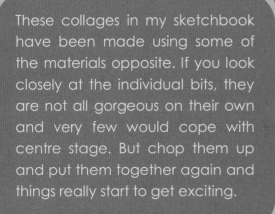

This pink and blue paper was actually where I scraped off spare paint on some baking parchment … but it is just the thing to give a contrast for the jugs

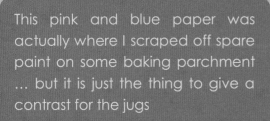

And here, notice what a difference those small white strips under the jugs make to the whole piece. They are really quite dull in themselves, but taken as a part of a whole, they become indispensable

The images on these two pages are made from a real mixture of materials - some real stars and others playing the equally important supporting roles. And the results are so exciting I think

This screen print worked well, but lacks a bit of impact, so I decided to go back into the image, starting with a white pencil to increase the contrast

However, there will also be some pieces that are so nearly there, but are just lacking something. Perhaps the dye washed out rather too enthusiastically. Maybe your crayon rubbing faded too much into the background or perhaps your overprint obliterated a very promising start.

Can we do anything to save these poor souls? You bet we can!! And it is such fun to do, you will view duffers with a sense of impending pleasure soon.

I like to use crayons and pencils to work back into these pieces. Look at your material and analyse what is not working and then work to change that.

Contrast definitely better, but I would still like to add a bit more – I think some gentle colour

Sometimes you need to deepen the colours and dark areas; sometimes lightening up and emphasising the light areas does just the job. Maybe some lines need extending or fattening or firming up, or loosening down. Maybe you need to add another layer of printing, or stamping, or stencilling to bring back an image you have lost.

Crayons and pencils can give results from very subtle and soft to a total transformation, so experiment and see what works best. Don't worry about messing up – you didn't much like this bit anyway, so view it as a safe place to experiment and practise.

I picked another piece of the plant, to just give me a few guidelines and added a light layer of pale green and yellow.

Not a huge difference, but a significant one and I am happy

I simply couldn't produce a whole book with hundreds of images and not include my much loved hound - Dixter. So here he is (left) on a piece which I made using rubbings - a rubbing pate of squares for the background and a rubbing from a stamp for the boy himself. We call him 'little dude' and I wanted to make a piece called 'Blue Dude' in homage to Matisse! It was

washed over with dye and I like it very much, but I have lost Dix a bit - he is not as blue as the title suggests to me.

So I went over him in both water resistant crayon and pencil to give him some impact and definition.

The pencil is really useful for working on the edges and adding a little detail, such as his collar, ear and eye.

I worked into the background with water soluble crayons to add some shadows and push the focal point out even more. I then worked over these with a wet paint brush to blend . I find this combination works really well for me,: I can blend my water soluble backgrounds, without worrying about the edges of my water resistant focal point bleeding. I am really happy with this piece now and it is ready to be stitched and made into a quilt. Maybe one day I will have an exhibition containing all the work I make featuring my animals!

Mixing it Up

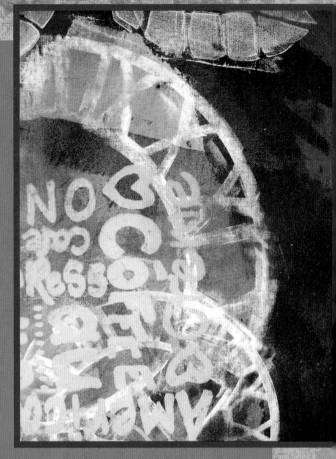

This may sound startlingly obvious, but always remember you have all these techniques at your disposal now, and they are not mutually exclusive! Sometimes a piece has all it needs with just one technique - this can be particularly true of feature or focal pieces. But for all your backgrounds and extras, mixing up techniques can often give much more interesting results. This is especially effective if you have made coordinating screens, stamps, stencils, plates etc. Keep assessing what you are doing and consider whether a change of technique is just what is needed. I like to keep all my made tools together in a file when I am working on a theme, then they are always easy to find and remind me whenever I am using them, that I have options. Later books in this series will be looking at working with various themes, so we will talk more about approaches for that when we get into those. Lots to look forward to!

This cloth (detail above) has rubbings, thermofax prints and stamps, in paint, crayon and dye. It both inspired the colour scheme and provided some key imagery for the quilt opposite

But for now, I have run out of pages and time, so I am going to stop. I hope you have both enjoyed and found this book useful and will join me again for our first theme ... which I think will be 'Coast' - yummy!

'Self 1: On Edge'

Books Books Books!!

There are so may textile books out there, I couldn't choose just a few. I buy loads and almost always enjoy them. But I will mention the following few, as being outstandingly gorgeous and also full of information. These are books you should really read as well as drool over and I think you will turn to them time and time again.

1.   If you want to learn the proper way to dye fabric, screen print and much much more, then you can do no better than get any or all of these books by Committed to Cloth (Claire Benn and Leslie Morgan) They cover everything in detail, give recipes and technical details, plus are also full of gorgeous and inspiring illustrations. They now come with free CD's too so you can watch the girls in action.

⇒   **Tray Dyeing: Exploring Colour, Texture & Special Effects**
⇒   **Screen Printing: Layering textiles with colour, texture & imagery**
⇒   **Thermofax Printing: Bringing personal imagery alive**

2.   As far as design and sketchbook work goes, I would recommend any of these books by Sandra Meech. Full of ideas and exercises to get you going and generously illustrated with examples from Sandra herself and lots of other artists.

⇒   **Contemporary Quilts: Design, Surface and Stitch**
⇒   **Creative Quilts: Inspiration, Texture & Stitch**
⇒   **Connecting Art to Stitch**
⇒   **Connecting Design to Stitch**

3.   Linda and Laura Kemshall need no introduction and are both talented artists. They are also skilled teachers and communicators and anything they write is always worth reading. Again, illustrations are always yummy too.

4.   If you like the idea of repurposed and recycled art, then get yourself this book by Cas Holmes. It is full of ideas for making your working practises greener and also wonderful examples of Cas and other artists work

⇒   **The Found Object In Textile Art**

5.   This book has been around for quite a while, but is invaluable for giving you ideas and inspiration for pattern making in your work

⇒   **The Textile Directory** by Karin Jerstorp and Eva Kohlmark

I also like to have a large collection of inspiration and reference books. A new theme nearly always suggests at least one new book to me. Here are some of my favourites ... pure eye candy really

⇒ **The Whimsical Works of David Weidman** - Davids' serigraphs and screen prints are magical

⇒ **Brian Cookes' Landscapes of Britain** - if, like me, you like the stylised type art posters of the 1930's to 1950's, then you will love this book

⇒ **London Transport Posters: A century of Art & Design**; edited by David Bownes and Oliver Green - more fabulous stylised art

⇒ **Sources of Inspiration** by Carolyn Genders - Carolyn is a ceramicist and this book is just brilliant for how to get inspired and then record that inspiration

⇒ **Print & Pattern Bowie Style** : books 1 & 2 - both books are heaving with wonderful inspiring ideas for pattern and imagery

⇒ **1950's Fashion Print** by Marnie Fogg   if you love this period like me, you will love this book

⇒ **A First Book of Na**ture by Nicola Davies and illustrated by Mark Hearld - no, not for your children, although they will love it too, but for the magical illustrations by Mark Hearld

⇒ **Mark Hearlds' Work Book** - prepare to be dazzled - one of the most beautiful books I own

⇒ **Art of the New Naturalists** by Peter Marren and Robert Gillmor - the covers of the New Naturalist books are rightly famous in their own right and are now collectors items. But you can see them all in this fabulous book

⇒ **Greek Myths** by Ann Turnbull and illustrated by Sarah Young - the myths are interesting but it was the stunning illustrations that made this book a must buy for me

⇒ **Charleston: a Bloomsbury house & garden** by Quentin Bell and Virginia Nicholson - started by Quentin Bell, son of Vanessa and Clive Bell, key figures in the Bloomsbury set, this book was completed after Quentins' death by his daughter Virginia. A fascinating read, and as you would expect, lots of pictures of the wonderful Charleston House.

⇒ **Natures Powers & Spells: Landscape Change, John Clare and Me** by Carrie Akroyd - a very interesting book in which Carrie finds a connection with the poet John Clare in their similar reactions to landscape change in their times. Beautifully illustrated with Carries art, and lots of John Clare poetry as a real bonus

I could go on for pages here, but that is enough to get you started I think! I haven't given publishers details, as these days it is very easy to find all such information online. I use Amazon extensively for book hunting and love their 'customers who bought this also bought' lists. Beware though—it can get a bit compulsive, although I can never see money spent on a books as anything other than a sound investment. Including this one I hope! Hope you enjoy some of these too.

Supplies

Art Van Go
The Studios, 1 Stevenage Road, Knebworth, Hertfordshire SG3 6AN
Tel: 0143 8814946
Website: www.artvango.co.uk
An aladdins cave of art supplies - watch the purse!

Fabric Guild
Kisko House, 48 Cobden Street, Leicester LE1 2LB

Tel: 0116 262 0569
Website: www.fabricguild.co.uk
Brilliant discounted fabrics including plain cotton

Kemtex Educational Supplies
Chorley Business & Technology Centre, Euxton Lane, Chorley, Lancashire PR7 6TE
Tel: 01257 23022
Website: www.kemtex.co.uk
All things dye

Crafty Notions
Unit 2, Jessop Way, Newark, NG24 2ER
Tel: 01636 700862
Website: www.craftynotions.com
All manner of stuff for the textile and paper artist - purse warnings apply here too!

Khadi Papers
Chilgrove, Chichester PO18 9HU
Tel: 01243 535314
Website: www.khadi.com
Yumbo papers and from a good ethical source too

Me!!
Hilary B: Original Art & Design
18 Mallard Close, Lincoln LN6 0RQ
Website: www.hilarybeattie.co.uk
I am now supplying many of the items mentioned in this book, so have a look at the website or visit my stand at the shows